Beautician Inspired

Amanda Sherie Wilcher

Illustrations by Blueberry Illustrations

To my daughter, Alanna Rose,
for constantly reminding me that I am strong.

To my mother, Rosa Lee, for her unconditional love
and a solid upbringing that never steered me wrong!

To all my sisters and brothers for the outpour of love,
support, and motivation that I could never repay!
To them all, day by day, I will try anyway.

**Mommy, Mommy, Mommy,
who or what should we be?
We've been thinking, thinking,
thinking *cosmetology!*

They like to paint faces,
nails, and toes.
There is so much more to beauty
and we want to know!

Do you have time, Mom,
to listen, listen, listen?
Please say yes, Mom!
Let us talk about beauticians.

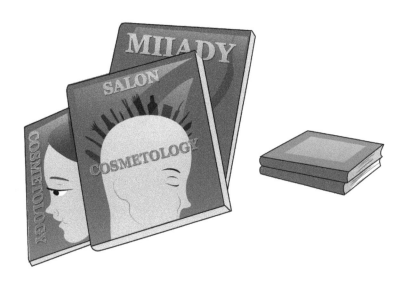

**Hundreds of hours of ideas,
practice, and books,
To test and become a professional
who helps people with their looks!**

From the top of your head
to the bottom of your feet,
A beautician can do it all
once you sit in their seat!

13

Beauticians are skillful
and it is a lot that they know,
Like doing ponytails and braids
to make your hair grow!

Heads in and out of the bowl,
brows, lips and chins clean,
Looking like a beautiful butterfly
that has spread its wings!

They wash and they wax,
but I am not talking about cars.
When they are all done,
people feel like superstars!

19

Their hands are able
to paint, sew, and style!
A passionate beautician
lets their imagination run wild!

Kings and queens all over the world,
A beautician can be a boy or a girl!

Practice, practice, practice
and ask for help too!
If you believe in yourself,
there's not one thing on this earth
that you cannot do!

Amanda Sherie Wilcher is a native of Wrens, Georgia. She completed her education at Jefferson County High School in Louisville, Georgia. Pursuing a career in the beauty industry, Amanda enrolled in Michaels School of Beauty and in 2009 received her diploma in the Cosmetology Program. She then enrolled in the University of Phoenix and graduated in 2013 with a Bachelor of Science in Business with a Concentration in Entrepreneurship.

After working successfully with SmartStyles Family Hair Salon as a leading stylist for two years and a manager for three years, she decided to step out in faith and begin her entrepreneurial journey.

Having her own salon "Diverse Creations Beauty Bar Express" for seven years now, being the CEO of her uniquely handmade "DCBBE Hair Growth Oil," her luxury hairline "Diverse Extensions," and her Feminine Care Line "Vaginal PH Pleasers," and now author of Beautician Inspired, Amanda has discovered her sense of purpose and power. She loves to read, write, research, and most importantly, execute. Her take on life is that anything she sets her mind to do, with faith and focus, it is done. This is her very first book but there are more than plenty to come.

For more information about her products, please visit
http://dcbeautybarproducts.patternbyetsy.com.

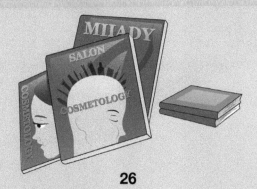